Places of Pride

The Work and Photography of Clara R. Brian

Places of Pride
The Work and Photography of Clara R. Brian

by Margaret Esposito
Photographs edited by Tona Schenck

McLean County Historical Society
Bloomington, Illinois
1989

McLean County Historical Society
Bloomington, IL 61701

© 1989 by The McLean County Historical Society

Printed by Illinois Graphics, typeset and bound by
Pantagraph Printing, all of Bloomington, Illinois

Cover design, Conley Art Studio
Photographic prints, I.A.A.—Graphic Production
Text editing, Martin Wyckoff

Book design—Tona Schenck and Greg Koos

Table of Contents

This book was a labor of friendship and love. It was undertaken with a sense of adventure to discover what was so essential to the development of an outstanding work, and with a sense of gratitude for a career that has been and continues to be challenging and rewarding.

Margaret Esposito
October 1989

Acknowledgments

Without the interest and cooperation of many people this book could not have been written. Their willingness to share knowledge and remembrances brought more depth of understanding than was available in the reports and news accounts, voluminous though these are.

The McLean County Extension Home Economics Program Council and Homemakers Extension Association Board provided the moral support and encouragement that such a task requires.

Also, it is most appropriate to recognize the work of two fine professional educators who caused the extension mission to have exceptional success and meaning in McLean County, Illinois: Clara R. Brian (adviser 1918-26, 1928-45) whose vision and dedication left a legacy and a challenge for those who followed, and Jean K. Lystad (adviser 1945-70), my valued co-worker, mentor and friend, who accepted the challenge and brought new dimensions of learning and living to the work.

In addition, it is essential to recognize some of my family who have helped to shape my life and career: my grandmother, Julia Sutton Mitchell, who taught me to find joy in words and ideas and who shared a deep commitment to lifelong learning; and to my mother, Gladys Mitchell Poulton and my children, Linda Kay and Stephen, who gave me the freedom and continuing support to take up the challenge of extension education in a premier county some 27 years ago.

To get a book like this on the press takes the efforts of many creative individuals. Loy Conley, proprietor of Conley Art Studio, not only provided the cover design but challenged the Historical Society staff to higher standards. The superb photographic prints were painstakingly pulled from the original negatives by the Graphic Production Department of the Illinois Agricultural Association. The printing was patiently handled by Larry "Lars" LaBounty of Pantagraph Printing. Martin Wyckoff, curator of the McLean County Historical Society, proofread the copy and assisted in the design.

Foreword

Don Munson
Station manager, WJBC Radio

What follows on these pages is proof we've been several times blessed here in McLean County. We have claimed as our own an extraordinary leader who arrived just in time to launch what became the largest home bureau in the entire nation. We were doubly lucky to learn she was also a darned good photographer and left for us a remarkable record of our lives two, three and four generations ago. And we were fortunate to latch on to a subsequent extension adviser whose interest, talent and energy were such that this book—this important piece of McLean County history—simply had to come to be.

Clara Brian became the county's first Home Bureau adviser in 1918 and gave it up in 1945, and during those years she helped bring Mclean County's rural home life a great leap forward. Times were changing rapidly. Horse power was giving way to mechanization on the farm. A demonstration of the new gasoline-powered tractors just outside Bloomington in 1916 drew 16,000 spectators. Organizations of farmers were forming. Meetings were being held, and the men who worked the fields were learning from each other.

But what about the homemaker? Many of the new methods of doing things weren't being applied to the domestic side of rural life. Clara Brian did more than anyone in McLean County's history to change that.

Miss Brian's Home Bureau meetings created an atmosphere of self-help among area homemakers as members began teaching each other. Her regular recipes in the Pantagraph were anticipated and were used. Farm families in Empire Township often sat down to a dinner identical to that being simultaneously enjoyed by families up around Money Creek—the result of a Clara Brian recipe in the paper the day before.

And the pictures she used in her teaching! What remarkable images of homemakers doing things the right way. The photos seemed to say "here is how you can be as progressive as your husband." They were positive photographs. People must have felt good viewing them then, and we certainly feel that way today.

Viewing them is something Margaret Esposito and the people at the McLean County Historical Society have been doing lately. Miss Brian left more than 500 negatives to the society, and they have been on a shelf for more than 40 years.

Here are nearly a hundred of the best of them, and I feel like I am looking at my own roots. I've a pretty good collection of pictures of the Munson family taken during this same era—most of them unlabeled, but many of them set on the old family farm near Randolph. My Aunt Dora Munson, a contemporary of Miss Brian, headed the home economics department at Bloomington High School for decades. These pictures tell me much about my own.

That is so thanks, in no small part, to the commentary provided by Margaret Esposito. Margaret has the historical perspective of someone who has spent more than a few winters in McLean County. (Do you remember the popcorn stand which stood decades ago just to the west of the old Irvin Theatre in Bloomington? Margaret was one of the vendors.)

Her work has been similar to Miss Brian's in so many ways. But the various media available to education have opened all kinds of possibilities, among them local radio. And that is where my association with Margaret began in the mid-1960s when I convinced her to air a daily report on WJBC. We called it "A Word for the Women" then, and broadened it to "Consumer Update" a few years later. Margaret still has a date with WJBC listeners each weekday morning at 11:45.

She has touched my own home many times over the years with information we have used—recipes, tips, health warnings, information on new products and prices. Margaret has made WJBC proud. She is an excellent extension adviser.

And now, thanks to her work in this book, we learn she is maintaining a tradition established long before.

A Farm Wife Remembers

My children had a working mother, only all the work was done at home.

We were up at 5:30 a.m.—my husband, the baby and I; the other children slept a while longer. The first thing to do was stir up the fire in the cookstove. This was our only source of heat for household warmth and cooking. One of the last chores before going to bed was to bank the fire in the stove, or it was a chilling morning and a delayed breakfast.

While Warren went to the barn to do the chores, I fed the baby and started breakfast. Although breakfast time varied depending on how much trouble there was out in the barn, I tried to have it ready when he came in. Our breakfast of oatmeal, bacon and eggs, toast and milk or coffee was ready when he came in. The children were up by this time, and we ate breakfast together; of course, no coffee for the children.

Then there was the busy time of packing lunches in the syrup buckets, and getting the children dressed and off to school. They walked the mile to school, so they had to leave in time to make the bell.

Kitchen clean-up and baby's bath were worked into that early morning time too. No running water in the house, no sink in the kitchen—dishwashing was done in a dishpan on the kitchen table, as was the baby's bath.

Next it was time to feed and water the chickens and, in the summer, to pick the vegetables for dinner. If it was winter, last summer's canning provided the vegetables, fruits and, quite often, the meat.

By noon, my husband was back in the kitchen for a hearty meal of meat, potatoes, vegetable and dessert—almost always a dessert. In the evening we would have a supper meal equally as large—hard work on the farm required a quantity of food for energy. Quite often the evening meal was made with the leftovers from the noon meal—you planned for that as a labor saver, but always there was a fresh salad at our table.

Of course, when we had a baby there was laundry to do every day, and the diapers required boiling occasionally. But whether it was once a day or once a week, the laundry was done with a washtub and scrub board, water drawn from the well and heated on the stove or a fire in the yard, and with homemade lye soap.

In the summer it was better to do the wash in a shady spot outside, and the clothes were hung on the line to blow dry in the sun. In the winter, the wash was done in the kitchen, and it was hung on lines strung throughout the house. All that scrubbing, wringing, dipping of water!

No two days were alike. You couldn't do much planning, but frequently I took a short rest (15-30 minutes) after the noon meal chores were done.

There was always mending to pick up, and the sewing machine was always open and ready. You know I made all the children's clothes and mine.

The house work was balanced with the garden and farmyard work. Planting, hoeing and harvesting, canning 600-700 quarts of food, tending the chickens, gathering the eggs, setting the hens so we could have a continuous supply of eggs and meat, and making the lye soap. Another busy time was when we butchered in the fall. Then we canned meat, made sausage, liverwurst, head cheese and scrapple. The lard was rendered to use for cooking and to pack the sausage in the crocks so it would keep.

I baked bread two or three times a week. And as I said, dessert was served almost every day. We didn't have electricity until much later. All the work was under my own power, no mixer, toaster, washer. Milk was cooled in the well and later in an icebox.

Why, you know, we only bought flour, sugar, and coffee from the store. We raised or made most everything we used.

It was a real treat to have the foods lessons and

recipes that Miss Brian brought to us. It helped me do a better job and gave me new ideas.

No inside plumbing meant a privy outside and a chamber pot under the bed. A washtub in the kitchen was the bath.

'Course, house cleaning in spring and fall, with carpets taken up and outside to be beaten, featherbeds aired, windows washed and everything.

Even in the 1920s, I was a go-for for my husband. I went on errands in town, first by horse and buggy; later when we bought a car, I drove.

There wasn't much time nor opportunity for social life. When you went anyplace you took the kids or stayed at home. At harvest time there was real hard work but sociability, too, for the neighbors helped out at haying, shucking and shelling—helped in the fields and helped with the meals.

The telephone party line gave you a way to socialize with those close by. When one person's phone rang (each of us had a special ring) everyone else knew who was on the line. Several of us could talk at the same time for a little chance to visit.

As we came to the evening hours, we made sure the fuel for the stove and the water for household use the next morning were in the kitchen and ready. These were chores for the kids as they were big enough.

Then it was off to bed for the kids, and I'd sit down with my knitting to relax before going to bed.

It was hard work, but I don't ever remember saying it was too hard to get done, and I wasn't sick hardly at all.

Interview with Mrs. Clara Dodson,
charter member of Money Creek unit,
by Margaret Esposito, October, 1989

The Work of Clara R. Brian

by Margaret Esposito

Miss Clara Brian, c.1935

Introduction

This book is about Clara R. Brian, home adviser to McLean County, Illinois, and the families with whom she worked in the years between 1918 and 1945. Most importantly, it presents a collection of her photographs, recording the conditions and the lifestyles of the families as they were and as they changed during those years.

The images chosen are for the enjoyment of the reader. Their aesthetic qualities have an intrinsic value and beauty. Their depiction of the times and people's lives have a charm, warmth and honesty that communicates simply and eloquently.

However, we must look beyond the picture to gain an understanding of the photographer, her work and her achievements. It is important to know about Miss Brian and the extension service which employed her.

Currently, I am serving in the adviser role which she pioneered, and I am the second person to have the position since Miss Brian retired in 1945. This in itself is a unique record for any county in the nation, just as she set a unique national record in 1926 when she completed eight consecutive years in a single county in the system.

During my seventeen-year tenure, I have had the experience of observing the breadth of her accomplishments and learning of the deep appreciation, even awe, which the people of the county feel for her work. The Home Improvement Association which she found in existence when she arrived later became the Home Bureau. With the support and active cooperation of the thousand-plus members, she developed the leaders of an organization that remains active in the county today as the Homemakers Extension Association. The organization still provides some of the financial and leadership support that Miss Brian found so effective in fulfilling her role as a countywide educator.

Development of the Extension Service

An educated citizenry has long been recognized as a vital component of a democracy. Early establishment of free public education, and a variety of educational movements in the United States were all designed to develop citizens who could function in an open political climate.

During the early years of the nation's development some influential citizens persisted in urging federal government involvement in agricultural education. However, the need was not filled until the second half of the nineteenth century.

In 1862, President Abraham Lincoln signed a series of three acts which addressed this concern. The Morrill Act was the enabling legislation for the creation of the land grant college system of agricultural and mechanical colleges; the Homestead Act opened new lands to settlement and farming, and a third act created the United States Department of Agriculture.

Later in the century, the Hatch Act established and funded agricultural experiment stations and the Second Morrill Act provided continuing funding for each state land-grant college. Thus the structure for the research, the university teaching components and the network for gathering the knowledge needed were in place.

Bulletins and annual reports were issued by the United States Department of Agriculture, and a variety of institutes and demonstration works were used sporadically to provide information. However, one last link of the system remained to be developed. Those who had little or no affiliation with the universities did not have access to the information on a continuous and usable basis.

In 1914 President Woodrow Wilson signed the Smith-Lever Act into law, stating that it was "one of the most significant and far-reaching measures for the education of adults ever adopted by the government."

In effect, the act established the delivery system to take the universities' expanding research-based information to the people. This method of education has been so successful that the extension service system has been widely adopted in other nations of the world, and especially in the developing countries.

The Smith-Lever Act created the Cooperative Extension Service as a part of the land grant college system with funding to be shared by federal, state and county sources. Specifically, counties in a state could request the services of an agriculturist and/or home economist if they agreed to provide the local support system and share the cost of the advisor's salary. Strong emphasis was to be placed on involvement of local people who could identify the needs to be met.

In the early years of the twentieth century these needs related to the accelerated rate of change from an agrarian to an industrial society, the increasing production of labor-saving devices, the construction of railroads and highways and the rural free delivery service. All were impacting upon the lives of families, and especially upon the lives of farm families.

The purpose of the law as stated by Congress was: "To aid in diffusing among the people of the United States useful and practical information on subjects relating to agriculture and home economics and to encourage the application of same."

Secretary of Agriculture David F. Houston characterized the provision of the act as nothing short of a comprehensive attempt to make rural life profitable, healthful, comfortable and attractive. He acknowledged that the intellectual and social sides of rural life could not be neglected, either.

In the beginning, there seemed to be some differences in audience focus. Agricultural advisers were some of the earliest staff hired, and as the provisions of the law were clarified, home economics advisers were employed. Home economists were needed, however, in both rural and urban areas.

In addition, world events influenced implementation of the new law. When the Smith-Lever Act was passed in 1914, Europe was just entering World War I. The United States's entry into the war in 1917 escalated the need for programs which the extension service had the potential to provide.

A shortage of farm workers, the demands of feeding and clothing the troops, shortages of foods at home, and a need to adjust lifestyles to cope were challenges to the whole nation. Those who lived in town were feeling the effects of war too, so home economics advisers had a role to fulfill with all residents of the county. In Illinois there were home advisers working in Chicago during the war years, but their services were discontinued after the war.

Extension Comes to McLean County

By 1915, the household science department of the University of Illinois had a state leader of extension on staff, and educational programs were being provided throughout the state via movable schools, farmers' institutes and lecture demonstrations. The value of such information being made available was recognized and there was a general awakening to the further advantages of having a home economist located in individual counties. By 1915, Kankakee County, Illinois had hired an adviser and they were developing a home improvement association. Mercer County followed that plan in 1917. In 1918, six counties organized, but in McLean County the enabling organization developed differently.

Mrs. Spencer Ewing of Bloomington had been appointed McLean County food chairman at the beginning of the war. In this role she experienced the lack of rural organization through which to accomplish the food conservation work. After being selected to serve on a state committee of the Council of Defense, she met Miss Isabel Bevier, head of the Department of Household Science at the University of Illinois. This relationship led her to a clearer understanding of the provisions of extension work and the Home Improvement Association.

Mrs. Ewing felt that such an organization would be very helpful in the food conservation work with which she was charged. She recognized the many benefits that

Mrs. Spencer Ewing, c.1935

would accrue to the county if a home economist could work with families on a full-time basis.

Her conviction grew, and Mrs. Ewing began to look at alternatives for starting a home improvement association in the county. An initial contact with the Household Science Club of Bloomington was an attempt to enlist the club's assistance in the project.

This visit was the beginning of a plan which culminated in the Home Improvement Association of McLean County being organized on a township basis.

Mrs. Ewing enlisted the aid of some of the Household Science Club members who lived in various townships of the county. Mrs. Barlow in Dry Grove, Mrs. Ed Coolidge in Normal, Mrs. Frank Benjamin in Bloomington, Mrs. Homer Johnson in Dale and Mrs. Hugh Stewart of Randolph townships were the original planning group. The first committee meeting was held on October 5, 1917.

The resulting plan was to organize each township for support of the Home Improvement Association, with a goal to recruit fifty members in every township who would each pay yearly dues of $1, or secure fewer members plus interested individuals and businesses willing to make contributions to total $50. For many years thereafter McLean County was known as the "$1 per member" county, and despite comments and coercion about increases, the county maintained a posture of low membership fees to encourage the greatest number of members possible.

Several meetings were held, and township representation increased. The January 17, 1918, meeting was a boost to morale. Although a membership campaign was not to begin until February 4, the committee learned that there were already 375 members on the roll. The minutes of the meeting read, "Mrs. Hugh Stewart reported 30 members and much interest."

By April 10, the names of four candidates for the position of home adviser had been received. Having enrolled 1,500 members by April 13, the group formally organized. Mrs. Spencer Ewing was elected the first president of the McLean County Home Improvement Association. The executive committee was directed to incorporate under the state laws of Illinois.

The committee also moved rapidly in the hiring process. Minutes of the deliberations seem to indicate a special preference for the candidate who had Illinois beginnings. Committee members referred to her as "our Illinois girl." The selection was made and the memorandum of agreement to match the $1,500 of the University of Illinois Cooperative Extension Service was promptly signed.

Therefore, when Miss Clara R. Brian began her work in McLean County, the association of 1,500 members was in place, it had negotiated an agreement with the Chamber of Commerce for office space, transportation was being arranged, and the home adviser could assume her vital role of teaching.

The classroom for extension work was the largest county in land area in the state, with a population of some 68,000. Approximately 25,000 county residents lived in the Bloomington area. The objective was to reach as many of the people as possible.

On June 1, 1918, Clara R. Brian started meeting with the township units. She taught from the Emergency Food Program on the exchange foods. In June, the members learned about "Wheatless Bread"; July's topic was "Meatless Dinners," and August information was on "Sugarless Desserts." All of these topics were of vital importance because of the wartime restrictions and shortages.

By September Miss Brian initiated another major program thrust, related to foods and nutrition. In the years that followed, the relationship between good health and good nutrition has continued as a strong interest for county programs.

Years after Clara Brian's retirement, Dr. Gertrude Kaiser interviewed Clara concerning her years in McLean County. At that time Clara gave credit for the rapid start and noteworthy success of extension education in McLean County to the Home Improvement Association and its leaders.

Clara R. Brian
McLean County Home Adviser

Miss Clara R. Brian was the first home adviser in McLean County, Illinois and she held that position for 25 years. Her influence as an adult educator was so far-reaching that in 1989 she is still remembered with respect and affection.

Whether reading reports of the period or visiting with those who remember Clara Brian, many of the same value-laden words are used to describe her. She was progressive, caring, knowledgeable, fair, dedicated, honest, firm and hard working.

Miss Brian is fondly remembered by those who knew her in a variety of roles—Miss Brian the home adviser, the boss, the Sunday School teacher, the landlord, the friend, my aunt. She is held in high esteem as women remember, sometimes in awe, how she brought the knowledge they did not have and helped them to apply it in ways which improved their lives and those of their families. Her life was one of service, a genuine dedication to the people of "her" county.

Clara R. Brian was the middle child of seven children, born to Frederick and Margaret A. Milligan Brian on October 20, 1876, in Lawrence County, Illinois. A few years after her birth the family moved to West Salem, then to Grayville where Clara graduated from a three-year high school in 1896.

One time she wrote that when she was quite young she loved the out-of-doors and running, sans sunbonnet, in the sun. Her mother sometimes threatened to sew the bonnet on her, for a pale complexion was thought more suitable for a girl. She admitted to the nickname "Tomboy" in those years.

Later the family moved to San Jose, Illinois, where Clara spent her early adult years. When the youngest child was nine, their mother died, and Clara assumed the responsibilities for home and family. Any plans that she may have had for continuing her education were delayed. But homemaking did not occupy all her time nor limit her horizons.

During the years in San Jose, Clara and her sister Cora opened a millinery shop. In some way, which is not entirely clear, the two young women changed from hat shop proprietors to newspaper publishers.

They published the San Jose Journal for a period of time. The paper was a four-page weekly for which Clara hand–set all the type. This was a task in which she became very proficient.

Her nephew Fred Brian recalls that she gave him his first instruction in type setting, and he incorporated that skill into his professional life as an artist. On the day he was interviewed he had been working in his studio where he still does printing, as well as printmaking.

Ultimately, Clara's plans for a university degree were delayed until 1911 when the youngest boy married and her sister was planning marriage and would be able to care for their father. That summer Clara renewed her plans to attend college.

A strong desire and a deep faith were taken with her as she left for Bloomington and Illinois Wesleyan University. Clara had enough money to pay tuition, but she would need to work for her living expenses.

An autobiographical sketch notes that: "The first proof of her faith was to find that, without her knowledge, the Kumler Scholarship had been secured for her use by a friend."

During her sophomore and junior years she worked for her room and board, and she earned enough as an assistant in the general chemistry laboratory and then in the food chemistry laboratory to pay her lab fees during her junior and senior years.

In 1915, Clara completed a bachelor of science

degree in home economics from Illinois Wesleyan University. A fellow student remembers her as being somewhat older than the others in the department, as indeed she was.

That student, Earlma Jones Kraft of Normal, also recalls that Clara helped her secure her first position at Rhode Island State College, where she worked in an extension-type program in the city of Providence.

The 1938 McLean County Home Bureau *Cookbook* dedication page notes that after graduation from Illinois Wesleyan, Clara R. Brian became head of the home economics department at Wesleyan University, Salina, Kansas. Miss Brian wrote that she "arrived in Salina, Kan, Sept. 1915, and found a Calumet Baking powder cookbook, the only related article on which to build a Home Economics Department at a University level. With the cooperation of the faculty and the University Friends the equipment was purchased and installed." Prophetically, the money for the equipment came from a University Friends group of one thousand women who paid a membership of one dollar each.

The three years Miss Brian was in Kansas were very productive ones. She developed the four-year course of study, equipped the department and wrote the high school home economics curriculum used in the Kansas schools.

During the summers after graduation from Illinois Wesleyan, Miss Brian started a master's degree program at Columbia University, New York City. She took a two-months' leave from McLean County in the summer of 1919 so she could complete her M.A. degree in nutrition and dietetics.

Arrival in McLean County

A *Daily Pantagraph* article of June 15, 1926, described Miss Brian's arrival in McLean County thus:

"In the summer of 1918, when conservation [of] food was constantly talked, Miss Brian wrote to this county, asking if there was anything that she might be able to do during vacation along that line. As a consequence, she came to this county and when she was made to see the need of such an organization as the home bureau and saw its possibilities, being Clara R. Brian, imbued with the pioneer idea of service and the establishment of new fields she stayed. The fact that her knowledge of extension work was limited and biased when she came, and that immediately she was informed concerning it, she accepted it as her work is another indication of the open-mindedness and farsightedness of Miss Brian's character."

June 1, 1918, was the starting date for her employment contract, but while Miss Brian was vacationing at her family home in San Jose she offered her services to the county to work with the food conservation program that was underway in wartime. People were strongly committed to conserving food to feed the boys overseas, and they were coping with shortages and rationing of familiar staples.

In May, Miss Brian wrote to Mrs. Ewing to tell her she planned to come to the county to see a scheduled cottage cheese demonstration which was to be presented by a conservation demonstrator. She requested that a county map with township lines be made available at that time, for she wanted to do some planning before her starting date in the county.

And so Clara Brian returned to McLean County. She took a room with Mr. and Mrs. E. C. Meeker at 6 White Place, Bloomington, and for 14 years she remained in this living arrangement.

In the mid–1930s Miss Brian bought a farm, but it was not until August 1947 that Miss Brian moved into a home of her own, at 204 East Walnut, Bloomington. Prior to moving in, the attic was remodeled into a four-room apartment which she rented to Miss Anne Meierhofer, dean of students at IWU.

People who knew her during her retirement years say that she enjoyed this home. Mrs. Scott Harrold, who lived on her farm all the years Clara owned it, says that anyone who went to visit her after 10:30 in the morning would have to plan to stay for lunch.

Miss Brian would insist that they stay, and she always had a variety of homemade "TV dinners" to heat and serve. Guests would have a choice of roast beef, roast pork, chicken, and more.

Fred Brian describes his Aunt Clara as a rather plain looking woman, but very bright, sensitive and perceptive. She was very typical of his female relatives—career oriented and not interested in marriage. He remembers her putting all of her energy into whatever she was doing.

Clara was the central figure of the family. Fred remembers her siblings as always appearing to consult with her or defer to her decisions, a source of some irritation in the family at times.

When Clara was about 90 years old, she took up oil painting. She was a realist in her art. Her nephew gave her some instruction, but she had much natural talent. In his opinion as an artist, she had more drawing ability than Grandma Moses, but she lacked something in color sense.

She spent some time in the extended-care wing at Brokaw. Fred visited his aunt frequently, and he always found her a stimulating conversationalist. There was never any idle talk; their conversation ranged from politics to current events and discussion of interesting ideas. They always enjoyed each other's company.

Clara wrote in an autobiographical sketch: "When she [Clara] was eight years old, she was converted and joined the Methodist Episcopal Church and never doubted the sincerity of that change that took place in her life at that time. A Christian home with the family altar influenced her life and her work."

Fred remembers his aunt as a deeply religious person. He recalls her chiding the rest of the family because they did not show the same dedication.

Clara would work six days a week and was totally dedicated to that work, but Sunday was a day to be observed.

She taught a young adults' Sunday School class at Wesley Methodist Church in the 1930s. She was very devoted to the group and very interested in the home and the nurturing of children in the home. Mrs. Harry Johnson was a member of that class, and she recalls that Clara was "just as interested in our children as we were."

The Harrold family also found that dimension in Miss Brian. She was like a grandmother to their two boys. And one late joy was the arrival of a namesake. One of the Harrolds' sons named his son Brian. The child was born while Miss Brian was still in the hospital, and she did get to hold him before he went home.

Clara Brian died on July 10, 1970. She left an exceptional legacy of service and accomplishment. At the time of the 20th anniversary of the McLean County Home Bureau, the Pantagraph article stated, "Through her untiring and efficient supervision the McLean County organization has gone to first place in membership and program accomplishments in the United States."

The Challenge to Change

When Miss Brian became the first home adviser she had the challenge of moving an organization from the written contract to the reality of a unique educational vehicle. This would permit her to provide information and experiences which would improve people's lives and help them change their lives as they moved into an industrial society.

Every organized township unit was visited during each month of the summer of 1918, and by September Miss Brian had plans for a program thrust that would involve more than just the Home Improvement Association members. As had been promised, the home adviser would work with everyone.

Even so, when the war ended in November of that year there were those who thought that the educational service was a wartime measure only. They were to learn differently. Miss Brian had brought to the county work an extraordinary dedication and a philosophy which reflected the progressive influence of Marion Talbot of the University of Chicago.

Travel A Challenge

The Home Improvement Association was to furnish the transportation for the adviser. So as soon as Miss Brian was hired, Mrs. Ewing wrote a letter to Mr. Bert Hawk, a member of the Rotary Club, telling of the new women's organization and the work they were proposing to do. She stated that the association would have the services of a home adviser to help the women and families of the county, and since they would soon have 900 members in the county and 600 in Bloomington-Normal an automobile was needed for the people to be adequately served. She further pointed out that although the 1,500 members paid a one dollar yearly membership,

Home Bureau Ford, 1919

the services of the adviser would be available to all the citizens of the county.

Mr. Hawk responded in a letter dated June 14, 1918, that "We are all mighty glad to have this privilege to co-operate in this good work."

For the first month, if the meeting place could not be reached by train or traction service, one of the members would come to Bloomington and take the adviser to the meeting and another would bring her home.

The automobile, a 1918 Ford, was delivered to the office at the Durley Building on July 5, donated by the Rotary Club. Years later, Clara wrote: "The adviser did not know how to drive a car but after an hour of instruction by a demonstrator, she was ready for the first trip in the new car."

However, the third component, roads to travel on, still left much to be desired. And for this new form of adult education the ability to reach county residents where they lived was considered essential. The fact that McLean County is the largest in land area in the state made this commitment a special challenge, and one Miss Brian commented on frequently.

During the first ten years of the county extension program, there were fewer than 125 miles of paved roads, 350 miles of gravel road and 1,542 miles of dirt road in McLean County. Further, it is significant that these dirt roads were soft and swampy during six months of the year, and they were barely passable with a team of horses.

From memoirs written after her retirement, it is apparent the adventures of travel started immediately:

"Monday, July 15, was a memorable day. The meeting place was Bellflower—thirty-five miles away. There were no paved roads—just dirt. The county tuberculosis nurse, Mrs. Earl Cooper, went with me. The car was a Ford Coupe, 1918 model. With fear and trembling, we started on our journey to the southeast corner of the county. We hadn't gone far until it started to rain. The top was down. It had to come up. The shower was soon over; then we came to a part of the road under construction and a bridge was not there. It was necessary to drive down a steep embankment and up on the other side. Impossible? How did we know until we tried. Down and up without a mishap, with perhaps a little more confidence in driving ability. A little more driving and we were at Bellflower. Meeting over, ready to start to Bloomington, but the car would not start. A man came, by request, from the garage, gave a few whirls to the handle in front and we were on our way home. Everything seemed to be going fine. When we were a mile east of Downs, the car stopped. Well, what is the matter now? Nothing except there was no gas in the tank, and even Fords in those days would not continue on their way without gas. Gas stations were not open after five o'clock that summer. A quarter mile walk and I was at the home of an obliging farmer who sold me five gallons of gas and delivered it to the tank. This was our last interruption and we arrived in Bloomington tired but with a lot of good experience out of my first day with a car. My brother [Dr. F. W. Brian] acknowledged to Mrs. Cooper a few days later that he was much relieved when he heard my voice over the phone saying we were safely home."

A record of repairs on the first car are somewhat revealing. Repairing tubes, buying new casings and tubes, putting on curtains and chains, tightening fenders, straightening fender and crank, and installing a starter were among the repairs and adjustments which cost a total of $375.36 from July 1918 to November 28, 1919. Those miles on the road must have been rigorous duty as one jolted over the rough roads until the fenders were in danger of coming off, and the tires and tubes needed replacement and/or repair. Chains were standard equipment for 1918, but it is an eloquent reminder of the adverse road conditions. Travel in the open car was only slightly more comfortable with the addition of curtains, and this was before the era of heaters. Installation of a starter would seem like a major improvement, too.

After some years of driving experience, and fortified by a variety of successes related to travel, Miss Brian made Pantagraph headlines about a trip to Weston, on the northeast edge of the county. She described the event more succinctly in one paragraph:

". . . the day of one big snow storm. Coming from Weston and leaving Chenoa going southwest on 66, I was stopped and told to go back. The driver of the car said that there were twenty cars stranded because a car blocked the road and none could get through. I did not want to go back. I wanted to go to Bloomington. There were four new chains on the trusty Dodge. I knew the road and the shoulders of that particular part of 66. I pulled off the road to the right, passed all the stranded cars, and was the first of that group to reach Bloomington."

Many of her experiences read like the *Perils of Pauline*. Another time she wrote:

"I decided to leave the meeting as soon as I could get away and get home early. The ground was getting well covered with snow but I was congratulating myself that I would get home in good time. About one mile east of Barnes station (that was the road used in those days), the left front axle of the car dropped to the ground and the wheel went spinning down the road. I didn't know what to do, so I did nothing for a few minutes—just thankful I was not hurt. I walked to the second house before I found a telephone to call the garage in Bloomington for help. No it is not a monotonous life, but one full of challenges."

Home Bureau Dodge stuck one mile southeast of Brandtville, 1922

Not only stamina and a sense of adventure were involved in travel of the time, but Miss Brian's sense of humor was reflected in a quote about the ruts in the road:

"There were always little funny incidents to lighten the more serious side of the work. Getting stuck in the mud or sliding off the road into a snow bank was not funny at the time, but it did give one something different to think about. Then there were the "ruts." How I longed for the ability to write and for the gift of oratory that I might give a lecture on "ruts.""

Both the students and the teacher faced special problems for travel. Mrs. Dodson of Money Creek unit recalls the time her husband drove a team of horses hitched to a wagon from their home to the meeting place, stopping along the way to pick up the members who needed transportation that day. In this way they were able to overcome the obstacle of bad roads to attend their unit meeting. She did not, however, have a recollection of what travel had been like for the adviser on that occasion.

A survey reported at the June 1931 Home Bureau directors meeting had been taken at the previous February unit meetings. It provides a unique insight into the commitment to the importance of the Home Bureau to those involved.

There were 455 people in attendance at the unit meetings, and they had traveled a total of 1,694.5 miles to be at their respective meetings. This was an average of 3.7 miles, with the longest distance traveled 15.5 miles. By contrast Miss Brian had traveled 946.8 miles that month as she visited all the units.

Weather and road conditions permitting, Miss Brian kept all her appointments with township units. Members recall her arrival in her little Ford, and they also remember many times of trial in the process.

Other times the home adviser traveled by rail, either the Interurban or the appropriate railroad. She would be met at the station or rail stop by an auto or a buggy and taken to the meeting place. On these occasions she may have stayed overnight or been transported to the next unit meeting, and then conveyed to the nearest station to return to Bloomington. Between June 1918 and April 1919, Miss Brian reported a total of 4,654 miles traveled, 3,354 miles by auto and 1,300 miles by rail. In her March 9, 1919, report she commented:

"Work out in the county is held up on account of the road conditions. It is almost impossible for people to get to the meetings, and I can only go where the meeting can be reached by train or when they come after me. Hope these conditions will soon be over and the work will move along smoothly."

The Ford roadster was replaced by a succession of Dodge Brothers vehicles. In some of the reports, the purchase of a closed car and, later, having a model equipped with a heater were pointedly noted.

When the Ford was replaced in 1920, the Home Bureau assumed the responsibility for the cost of the new auto and for all the subsequent cars used by the home advisers until the 1950s.

It is natural to assume that much of the success of extension education in the 1920s and 1930s was the ability to take the information to the people because of improved roads and automobiles. Meeting with people where the changes were to take place was a major strength of the program.

Developing the Program

Two small desks and three chairs in the front reception room of the Association of Commerce and the Farm Bureau was the first office of the Home Improvement Association. Until that time, Mr. Dave Thompson, farm adviser, and Mr. Heber Hudson, secretary of the association, shared the second floor suite in the Durley Building at Main and Jefferson streets in Bloomington.

During those first weeks, members of the Home Improvement Association volunteered secretarial time until a half-time secretary was employed.

Because there was no schedule to follow, it was decided that the township units would be visited as they found a place to meet and set a time commensurate with the adviser's schedule.

Mt. Hope Township was the first to request a meeting, and on Wednesday, June 5, Miss Brian presented her first lesson to a unit. And for all the years that followed, that unit continued to meet on the first Wednesday of each month.

As other townships firmed their June schedules, the adviser met with them. Every organized unit was visited each of the summer months that year.

Wartime restrictions on the use of wheat flour were making changes in the established patterns of food preparation. The homemakers were having a difficult time making bread from other flours, so the first lessons were on using these substitutions in breadmaking.

Demonstrations were, and still are, a preferred method of information delivery in the homemaker units. Many members recall the bread demonstration work which Miss Brian did.

She would arise early to prepare the dough and start it on the first rising. Then she would pack the ingredients for two more batches of dough. The active yeast dough would be packed properly to aid in the rising process, and all would go into the car.

Some place along the route, she would stop, punch down the dough and start it on the second rising. Arriving at the meeting place, everything would be set out for making a second batch of dough. This was to be used in the next demonstration of the day. The dough which had been set early in the morning was then formed into loaves or other appropriate products, and it was ready for the oven. Thus the whole process was presented to the audience in about one hour.

Getting back in the auto, she would be off to repeat the process for the afternoon unit meeting.

Miss Agnes Huth, office secretary for many years, recalls helping her with the demonstrations. She would arrive at the office about 7:00 a.m. and she and Miss Brian would assemble and prepare the components of the demonstration of the day. They would load the car and be on their way. When they arrived at the meeting place, Agnes would set up the demonstration materials. Miss Brian would present the lesson, then Agnes would pack up the baskets, and they would be off to the next meeting.

Remembering further, Agnes said they sometimes came back to preparation of a dinner meeting for some group or committee. Lacking that commitment, Agnes might work at her secretarial duties until 10:00 or 11:00

p.m.

A work week was six days, and the hours varied. They were not just eight hour days.

By the end of the first year in McLean County much work was underway. The Home Improvement Association had indeed been moved from an enabling organization to an action-oriented association. The name had been changed to McLean County Home Bureau, the membership had grown to 1,535 members, and a five-part program was in place.

Program Options

The five areas of study were "Conservation and Consumption," "Health and Sanitation," "Accounting," "Equipment and Household Management," and "Textiles." Within each of these courses of study there was a series of lessons prepared to be presented at monthly unit meetings. Each unit discussed the options, and then they selected a course of study for the year. The adviser and local leaders shared the responsibility of presenting the lessons in the units. Additional pertinent topics were included in the monthly programs through minor lessons which were presented by volunteer leaders. This provided a variety of educational materials to meet the local members' needs.

By this time Miss Brian had developed a schedule of teaching which placed her in the units for approximately four days per week, and two days in the office. Saturdays were devoted to what she called "subject matter," department workshops and directors' meetings. Of course weather, travel conditions and health modified this plan or restricted the attendance at these meetings.

Experience and some experimentation modified the meeting schedule over the early years, but by 1926 the plan of all-day meetings for each unit, and the adviser meeting with each unit for half of the day was the one most workable. This continued for many years. Even in the 1980s a modified version of this plan is still in use, so the homemakers may have a twelve-month program of education.

In October of 1920 Miss Brian logged 1,201 miles in automobile travel during 18½ days in the field. Only 7½ days were spent in the office. With all this effort, a very strong and growing organization was developing.

Despite this rigorous schedule a monthly bulletin was developed as another means of communication. In addition, the adviser met with community clubs, parents' organizations, and Illinois State Normal University and Illinois Wesleyan University home economics students. From the beginning Miss Brian was adviser to the county.

In some cases the women's editor of the Daily Pantagraph would attend the meetings and report them in depth. The on-going relationship with the Daily Pantagraph became a major facet of Miss Brian's service to the county.

The YWCA food service benefited from her interest in management and sanitation work. Community involvement was extensive.

Today it is called networking, but in those early years it was an expedient way of getting the most accomplished in a major effort to help the people of the county. Miss Brian worked with the Day Nursery, the county health nurse, the McLean County Tuberculosis Association, the Red Cross health committee, the school principals and teachers, the county superintendent of schools, the Farm Bureau, the churches and any group that was interested in the welfare of the county's citizens.

Her perspective was broad-based. She thought of her work as the opportunity to bring the information gained in the laboratory and classroom to the homes of the county where it was needed and would be applied. This was the progressive era, and the Home Bureau proved to be an excellent vehicle for accomplishing the goal of a more healthful, rewarding lifestyle for more people.

Equipment and Household Management

Miss Brian's first annual report spoke eloquently in a few words and two pictures of a major concern for the farm women with whom she worked.

> "One picture was taken of a corn dump, showing how a load of corn can be put into the crib in five minutes time. This same farm had a windmill which pumped water to the stock in the barn yard, but there was no facilities for getting the water into the house except as it was carried in by the bucket full."

This set the tenor of a major program thrust in the next several years. A slide presentation prepared from photographs which Miss Brian took in homes throughout the county had special impact at unit meetings.

Titled "Household Equipment, The Reason Why," the pictures of kitchens and their arrangement, dining rooms, sanitary and unsanitary toilets, laundry areas, and machinery used on the farm highlighted the adviser's comments. Pictures of children were shown as the "reason why."

The conclusion was that "Every woman has a duty to her family, her neighborhood and her community, and must have her work made easier in order to give her time and strength for these outside privileges."

Five equipment tours were organized and taken in the fall of 1920. During four of these, 48 homes were visited in 28 McLean County townships. The fifth tour was to the Senator Dunlap home in Champaign County.

A total of 499 persons carpooled and traveled 457 miles for these educational events. The features of special interest at the many homes included lighting, heating, water plants, electric and gas mangles for ironing, power washing machines, vacuum cleaners, chemical toilets, portable smoke houses, kitchens, room arrangements in modern homes, dumb waiters and modern poultry houses.

Besides the several hundred women who had first-hand information about the newest equipment and conveniences, there were two additional results noted in the evaluation. The Home Bureau had become better known as a result of the publicity. And, a letter to the Bloomington Daily Pantagraph had directed criticism to the fact that only the most modern and expensive facilities were visited on these tours. This promptly resulted in another tour, of the home of a tenant farm family. Here, it was concluded that the homemaker had done an excellent job with what she had available.

Another countywide activity sponsored by the Home Improvement Association was "Household Equipment Week." All the merchants of the county were invited to have window displays of the newest equipment from their stock. The merchants reported an increase in sales because of this activity.

Later, household equipment loan kits were assembled. They included such small items as a spatula, a paring knife, a bottle sprinkler for dampening laundry, etc. Units which were studying the equipment learning module could request one of the kits for volunteers to use in their own homes. Each of the items was used for one week by the study group members. When they had in-home experience with all the small equipment in the kit, a report to the unit was made. They discussed usefulness, any limitations, and the value to homemaking. At any given time there were four kits in use in the county. Miss Brian stressed in this lesson that each homemaker had to know her own needs and devise her own plan of labor-saving devices and methods.

In her recommendations for household equipment, Miss Brian advocated water in every home, a power clothes washer of some kind, a mangle for pressing or a simplex iron, folding some clothes directly from the line, use of a dish dryer, and a written schedule of meals.

In April and May of 1920, Home Bureau members reported that they had purchased such items as a spatula, two bottle sprinklers, a tea wagon, an electric vacuum cleaner, a kitchen cabinet, two steam cookers, three fireless cookers, a paring knife, an aluminum cookware set for $65, and an electric plate, and equipped a laundry room and installed a bathroom. These equipment changes were attributed to the recent emphasis on equipment and its relationship to family life and health.

In 1935 Miss Brian bought a farm in DeWitt County. The house on the property was in extremely poor condition, in fact virtually uninhabitable. Clara Brian the professional and Clara the farm owner held the same high standards. Her belief in sound management and equipment commensurate with the work to be done was unwavering.

Mr. and Mrs. Scott Harrold were hired as the tenants, with the understanding that they would have to wait for the house to be remodeled. Miss Brian assured them they would not regret waiting to move to the house on the farm. She reminded them that renovation was both slow and costly.

When the young couple moved to the farm home six months later, the house was habitable and it held the promise of much more. They found all the wiring and plumbing in place, so when REA reached their area it was a simple matter of bringing the water and electricity into the home.

Mrs. Harrold remembers Miss Brian as a landlord who was always interested in what was new and efficient on the farm and in the farm home. She was knowledgeable about farming and willing to make the necessary changes to improve the operation. Drainage tile was installed when it was apparent there was a need. As new equipment became available she encouraged them to invest in it.

Of equal interest was the equipment for the home. A pressure canner and the tin cans for preserving food were in the farm home at an early time. When the Harrolds were expecting their first child, Miss Brian insisted that an electric sewing machine was essential. This is not to imply that all this was furnished to the tenants, for Miss Brian's practical nature helped her to understand that it would not be in the family's best

interest to do this. But her knowledge and influence encouraged creating the best farm life possible.

Clara's philosophy of fairness and concern was evident even in her relationship with her farm tenants. While she owned the farm she wanted it to be representative of her values and concerns. And, when she was ready to sell the farm she made it possible for the Harrolds to buy the property, for she did not want anyone else to own it. Presumably she wanted the progressive farm and home life to continue.

Health and the '20s

"Then came October [1918] and the never-to-be-forgotten flu epidemic," wrote Clara Brian. The focus of the program changed abruptly. It was a health issue, but it was not an academic subject.

Miss Brian continues: "All programs were discontinued. Home Improvement Association members, city and county, joined with women of other organizations to help care for the sick. Monday, October 14, I began work as dietitian of the Emergency Hospital set up in the Bloomington Country Club. A fine group of women joined with me in preparing and serving food to the sick and to all the doctors, nurses, and nurses' aids who so willingly gave of their time and strength to this emergency work. The Home Improvement Association units of both farm and home organizations furnished most of the food. All kinds of vegetables, milk, butter, chickens, eggs, etc. came in abundance from all parts of the county. During the two weeks, 3,600 meals were prepared and served. One hundred and fourteen patients were cared for by the doctors and nursing staff. Four of the patients died; only two of those who worked at the hospital took the disease and they had light cases. Again, the organization had proven to the communities the value of a rural people organized."

The crisis passed, November was a month devoted to returning to normal living and planning. The Home Improvement board profited from the experience and elected to give major emphasis to a well-organized course of study on food and health.

Reviewing the lessons and reports, one is struck by the importance which was placed on nutrition, exercise and sanitation as it related to health. It is something of *deja vu*, with America's current revival of commitment to this triad.

As was noted earlier, the newest in foods and nutrition was a major program area, and it was integrated into the emphasis on healthful lifestyle which permeated Miss Brian's teaching. This was readily related to overall health with an early emphasis on sanitation in households, and on farmsteads through a countywide crusade against rodents and flies.

In her efficient manner, Miss Brian organized a comprehensive program around a pest extermination drive. The Home Bureau members received instruction in the health dangers and how to maintain the best home standards. The school children were given education through programs and bulletins.

By April 1920, there was a program in the schools with a slogan of "Bat the Rat, Swat the Fly, Rouse mit the Mouse." School children presented playlets on the subject, and positive action was encouraged. Miss Brian noted that children do better when teacher and mother cooperate, and she felt that the area of health and sanitation was a community affair that should involve everyone.

An extermination drive in each township was sponsored by the Home Bureau. The county organization offered a $5 prize for the township reporting the largest number of rodents killed. Each of the township units was encouraged to hold a drive, and to offer cash prizes for the family in the township which killed the most rats and mice.

Weston unit held a strawberry ice cream social to raise the money for their prizes. They reported a profit of $35 from the event, but it was not reported whether the entire amount went to the rodent drive. Other units held a variety of events to raise money.

Twenty-three townships reported 40,372 rats and mice killed, but equally important was the educational impact of this major drive. The county residents had learned the importance of eliminating insect-carrying pests, and they continued to work on the problem.

Another phase of the countywide health emphasis was the elimination of the breeding places of flies. In all of these efforts Miss Brian used a variety of methods to get her message across: articles in the Daily Pantagraph and 17 county newspapers, distribution of federal and state bulletins, distribution to school children of 1,000 Illinois Health Department bulletins, and speaking to community groups including parent/teacher organizations and joint Farm Bureau and Home Bureau meetings. Education and involvement brought results.

By August of 1920, lessons on healthful exercises for the homemaker had been given, and 414 women had agreed to follow the daily regimen of health specialist Fannie Brooks's exercise chart.

Organized recreational events, both in the units and countywide, were planned. Camping for farm women became a regular activity after the first year at Camp Lantz, which was in the western part of the county along the Mackinaw River. The camp program included swimming, boating, games and contests. Drama and campfire programs were special events. Morning flag raising and vesper services punctuated the beginning and the ending of the days. This was recreation and renewal for the members.

If every woman had an obligation to the school, then Clara Brian must have felt that her obligation was to enhance this relationship and secure positive action.

A letter to 30 Home Bureau health chairmen urged them to appoint a woman in each school district to provide leadership to a cooperative program with the public dispensary and the Red Cross. The major objective was to provide physicals for the public school children. This was a very successful and beneficial project.

Miss Brian reported in July of 1920, that 2,112 Child

Home Bureau exercise lessons, 1935

FOOT EXERCISES—To Strengthen Arches and Stretch Leg Tendons— 1. Seated as in Fig'r H with towel looped under metatarsal arch of left foot, extend left leg straight or heal leading, knee straight and pull towel taut. Grip toes hard over edge of towel, pulling harder with right hand, so the foot is rotated inward.

Labor Bureau bulletins were mailed to 435 families with 524 children.

Part of the health curriculum offered to the Home Bureau units was home nursing, but at first this did not seem to be a program that was chosen by many of the groups. Reports indicated that individuals called for this information as needed.

Accounting and Management

McLean County's success in introducing homemakers to an accounting program received national acclaim. By 1939, some county residents had kept home accounts for 20 years.

The accounting system was developed at the University of Illinois by state specialists, and each year the books were sent to the state for evaluation. The account keepers received a written report plus a summary of data from the aggregate of all books submitted.

In 1936, a seven-part series on homemakers who kept accounts with the University of Illinois system featured Miss Lavon Kinsey of McLean, Mrs. Peter Ropp of Normal, Mrs. Harry G. Johnson of Normal, Mrs. Arthur Wehmeier of Stanford, Mrs. E. D. Lawrence of Bloomington, Mrs. George Condon of Carlock, and Mrs. Park Kerbaugh of Allin Township. Featured with some of the account keepers were the two office secretaries, Gertrude Bird and Agnes Huth, who had the yearly task of forwarding the account books to the university.

Accounts were quickly recognized as one part of a larger management picture, and other programs incorporated a management section. Homemakers were encouraged to write out menus, canning record sheets were distributed so a total of foods preserved could be reported, and millinery class participants did cost comparisons on hats made as opposed to ready-made.

Because the care of chickens was most often delegated to the farm wife, Miss Brian initiated lessons on management of the flock. This was recognized as a "new phase of the Home Bureau work," and it began with the culling of the "slackers."

When the stories of this lesson start, so do the smiles. It was not an academic exercise, but a demonstration in the farm lot.

As a result of one lesson, a flock of 96 penned chickens was culled. The homemaker reported that 38 of these were identified as slackers, laying 1 egg in five days. The remaining 58 chickens laid 43 eggs in five days. Record keeping of this kind had real meaning for the keepers of the flocks. They could move from that understanding to an appreciation for other types of account keeping, but not everyone expanded the record keeping, preferring to concentrate on the poultry accounts only.

The value of the demonstration method of teaching, as used so successfully in Home Bureau work, is apparent in another anecdote about chicken culling.

A young woman who had responsibility for the care and feeding of chickens on the family farm had seen the culling demonstration. Later she heard the report of the Home Bureau member whose flock had been culled. When she went home and announced she was going to follow this new practice, her father objected. She culled the flock, however, despite his remarks. When she had demonstrated the success of increased production, the father became a strong advocate of the practice.

Miss Brian's tenure in McLean County spanned two world wars and the Great Depression. With the World War I years behind her, she planned and educated to help the people through the changing postwar years. Then when the economic crisis came, she retooled and began to work with thrift and scarcity.

In the depression years, families needed new sources of income. When farm families were burning corn for heat because there was no market for their crop, the Home Bureau and Miss Brian began to look at ways of getting other products to market.

The Home Bureau organized a farmers' market in the first floor of the Farm Bureau building at the corner of Center and Monroe streets. Many families sold butter, eggs, dressed chickens, baked goods, etc. through this outlet.

When it became necessary to candle the eggs for sale to the public, Miss Brian taught this technique to the homemakers. This allowed the women to continue to market their eggs.

Gladys Rhoades of the Hudson unit was a charter member of the organization. She recalls her last week at the farmers' market. Two churnings in that week yielded 72 pounds of butter. All of it was worked, formed into pound blocks, and wrapped in butter paper to be marketed.

Another time she remembers dressing 24 fryers to sell. She started with gathering the flock by feeding them some corn. Then, using a long wire with a hook on the end, she caught the 24 chickens, killed them, and dressed them. This was done between 2:00 and 6:00 the afternoon before market day. The dressed chickens were stored in the ice chest overnight.

Another Home Bureau venture which met with considerable success was a lunchroom in downtown Bloomington operated by the Home Bureau. The food service was opened in the front part of a store in the beginning, and later moved into a separate rented location.

A manager was hired for the business, and the food was prepared by the members and placed on consignment in the shop. Lunches and dinners were served six days a week, and the downtown workers found it a great convenience.

Helping families through innovative programs was typical of Clara Brian's approach to Home Bureau work.

Textiles

"Textiles" was the umbrella title which included lessons on clothing for the family and interior design. By 1921, 15 of the township units had completed a course of study which included making and hanging of curtains and clothing construction. Demonstrations and workshops made these courses very practical.

Over 50 women had made their own dress forms at county workshops within the first year of the program.

This was an all-day project, which was a large investment of time for a homemaker. But the result was a relatively inexpensive sewing aid, something usually not within the budget of the average woman.

Miss Agnes Huth, office secretary, described the rather tedious technique during an interview.

Construction started with the making of a base from a knit fabric tube which conformed to the model's figure. This base was then covered with strips of heavy brown paper applied on the human model. A process for gluing and stiffening came next, and then there was the drying time as the model remained immobile and in a standing position.

When the form was dry, the model emerged from the "cocoon" by having a slit cut up the center back. Rejoining the back slash with more paper strips and glue and placing the form on a stand gave the model a replica of her body on which to fit her garments. Of course, this assumed that she didn't change size!

Hats were an essential part of the wardrobe in the '20s and '30s, so hatmaking was included in the textile classes.

Hats made by Home Bureau millinery class, 1923

Starching
A. Effect on fabrics—Corn and wheat starch are in general used in the form of boiled starch, to stiffen a part or the whole fabric. Some parawax is often dissolved in the boiled starch to increase the gloss or smoothness of the fabric and to prevent the iron from sticking. Starch protects fabrics to some extent, since soil is not so readily absorbed into them. It takes longer to iron starched fabrics than unstarched ones.
B. Effect on personal comfort—Since starch closes the pores of the fabric, a starched fabric is hotter in summer than an unstarched one. Young children's clothing should not be starched in hot weather.
C. Recipe for laundry starch: Use 2 to 4 tablespoons to 1 quart of water. Mix a little water with the starch; then add the rest of the water. Bring to boiling point, stirring to prevent lumps. Add paraffin, melted. Thin with cool water, dip clothing to be starched.

Reports from participants in one of these first classes list the cost of making a hat from $2.50 to $3.95. One woman cited savings of $10.00 to $15.00 on one very fancy hat. What was most important, however, was that she was able to get a hat to fit her headsize, "something almost impossible before."

Girls' 4-H Club work started very early in McLean County, and by 1925 there were 19 clothing clubs with 212 members. The girls reported 815 garments made, 53 garments made over, 245 garments mended, and 220 stockings darned. Thirty-three of the girls were doing the family mending.

As the depression years gripped the Midwest, there was an increased emphasis on thrift. Several people still quote Miss Brian's philosophy: "Use it up, wear it out, or do without."

Lessons on fabric dyeing and remodeling clothing were in demand. One member reported successfully dyeing her husband's suit, and she expressed appreciation for having learned how to save so much money. Remodeling clothing and making clothes for the children from a man's discarded suit or woman's dress were other economies taught in Home Bureau classes.

In 1931, consumer and/or sewing skills were involved in the "One-dollar Dress" contest. This was a unit and a county competition which brought into focus many facets of consumerism and clothing construction. What the reports did not reflect was how difficult it was to secure the dollar to spend, or how many could not compete for lack of that sum of money.

Home decorating lessons were early favorites, and Miss Brian's philosophy of making the home more efficient and healthful provided additional emphasis when these courses of study were elected by a unit.

For those groups studying window treatments, a miniature window frame was used to demonstrate the correct way to measure and hang curtains or draperies. Miss Brian carried this equipment to the units so the members would have the visual instruction as well as the lecture.

Rug-making was another furnishings lesson, and at one time the Home Bureau had a loom which could be used by the members. Miss Huth recalls helping those who came to use the loom, and in some cases she actually wove the rugs from the cut strips which were brought.

Rug-making on Home Bureau loom, c.1936

In other years, decorative pottery was studied. Tours were taken to some of the nearby pottery factories including Morton and Lincoln. The visit introduced the women to the manufacturing process and provided the opportunity to see the newest designs, and, of course, to buy from the showroom.

Other years the presentation illustrated the historic development of kitchens, the newest in household equipment, and a variety of subjects that were meaningful to families. These events "gave opportunity for creative expression and getting acquainted with members from all parts of the county."

For the 25 years Miss Brian worked in McLean County she helped families and individuals to cope with the day-to-day tasks, and the environment in which those tasks were performed. People were encouraged to develop an interest and a belief in their ability to favorably alter that environment.

Household Equipment Display with electric ironer, c.1920-25

Countywide home and farmstead beautification contests were sponsored through the Home Bureau. A tour of the newly-landscaped gardens of Mrs. Spencer Ewing was held in conjunction with one such contest. Jens Jensen was the landscape architect. It was an excellent example of the contribution gardens and planned outdoor spaces can make to the home environment.

"Pageants of Progress" were presented on a bi-yearly basis. This was a means of reaching new audiences and to showcase the educational work of the Home Bureau.

Miss Brian described the pageant held in the Deere Building on South Main Street. The topic was "Artificial Lighting in the Home:"

"The display showed the light obtained from a cloth dipped in fat in a can, candles, kerosene lamps, etc. to the latest fixtures in gas and electricity. Needless to say, the public who passed by as well as the women who assembled the display knew more about interior lighting than they did before the pageant was held."

Pageant of Progress, December, 1921

Expanding Needs and Interests

As the Home Bureau developed and the members and county residents began to understand the capabilities of the organization, the program was expanded. Continuing education of the adviser and growth in the knowledge base created by ongoing research made possible the matching of extension programs to the needs of the county residents.

The Home Bureau organizational experience was developing excellent leadership among the members. It was time for a new program area called "Home and Community." Certainly, this was commensurate with Miss Brian's philosophy about women's roles outside the home.

In 1923, Miss Brian conducted 27 lessons on "Home and Community" with an attendance of 670 people, while Home Bureau members reached 255 members at 14 programs on the same topic.

"Home and Community" was described as one of the most popular courses given in the county. Topics ranged from laws affecting women and children to the value of clubs to the community. Special emphasis was given to the value of close cooperation between schools, churches and homes.

The Illinois Home Bureau and county affiliates were members of the Associated Countrywomen of the World. And when the international conference was held in Washington, D.C. a delegation of homemakers went from McLean County. The women were becoming citizens of the world as well.

Mrs. Lou Hartzold of Danvers recalls the trip with much enthusiasm. The overnight train ride, staying in a hotel for the first time, the contact with women of other nations, and meeting with Illinois legislators were exciting and beneficial experiences.

Women at work in the community could make a difference, the Home Bureau members learned.

Activities which would improve the rural areas were given special attention. So, when the Illinois Art Association announced a five-year campaign for

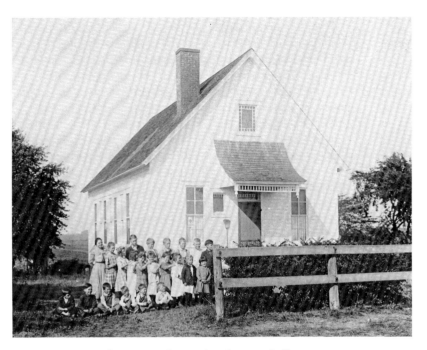

"Rose Hill spent $50.00 on their school grounds."

beautifying country school grounds, the McLean County Home Bureau was involved. Miss Brian took pictures of the rural schools in the county as the "before" pictures to document starting conditions. These were used later to evaluate the progress of the various schools.

A charter member of the McLean County Home Bureau commented that Miss Brian was always interested in foods and children. This became apparent as she focused on children and family relations in her in-service education. During September and October of 1924, Miss Brian took a vacation to observe the work being done in care and discipline of children at the Merrill-Palmer School in Detroit, Michigan. When she returned to the county, four classes for young mothers were organized. They had to have a child under six years of age, and a minimum of ten people in the group. The focus of study was "the training of the child physically, mentally, morally and spiritually."

Utilizing all resources available, the Home Bureau secured a scales from the Mead-Johnson Company. A program of weighing and measuring the children of women in the study groups was initiated. Resulting data was compared with charts prepared by the Illinois State Health Department. In a few cases where the children were underweight, appropriate diets were planned and discussed with the mothers.

Training of pre-school children was quite new in Illinois, and Clara Brian was the person who initiated this work. Perhaps this growing interest in child growth and rearing resulted in the adviser resigning her position in McLean County in 1926 to accept the Laura Spellman Rockefeller Memorial Scholarship to study child training at the University of Minnesota.

Her leave-taking message stated:

"Home Bureau Work in McLean County is getting on a good basis. The women are beginning to believe in the organization and to see its possibilities. The social side of Home Bureau work to them is worth all it costs, as it is the only organization financed by Federal Funds for women; and, next to the Church, the Adviser considers it the most important organization for women that has ever been organized."

Miss Esther Kahle succeeded Miss Brian, and the work continued for 15 months. However, ill health caused her to resign before completing two years as home adviser.

The Home Bureau organization continued the work for the next nine months. The board met regularly and countywide events were sometimes substituted for unit work. It was a period when the leadership which the women had developed was apparent, and it was put to the test in those months.

It must have been with great relief that Mrs. Simon Moon reported to the Home Bureau that she received a letter from Kathryn Van Aken Burns, assistant director of the home economics extension.

Mrs. Burns had met Miss Brian at a home economics meeting in Des Moines, Iowa. She learned that Miss Brian's study was completed, and, more significantly, Miss Brian did not have a position for the next year. Mrs. Burns indicated that other states were interested in employing Miss Brian, but she would like to see her back in McLean County. Miss Brian was returning to her home immediately after the conference, so they could reach her there. "I know she has always had a soft spot in her heart for the McLean County H.B." Mrs. Burns added.

And so Miss Brian returned to continue in the home adviser role she had so capably and carefully created.

A Sense of Safety

After her return to the county, Miss Brian initiated a study which would benefit families through an increased understanding of accidents in the home. It was another first for McLean County women.

A detailed study of home accidents was undertaken. This was done by distributing accident report blanks to the Home Bureau members. Their cooperation was requested, and they were to keep a record of any accident in which a physician was called or the victim was unable to work for more than half a day. The resulting data were the basis for some early farm safety statistics.

County pageants continued to be staged by the Home Bureau on alternate years. These were designed to showcase the work of the Home Bureau and to educate. Excellent cooperation from the Chamber of Commerce, local merchants, the Home Bureau units, and other facets of the community were reported. The events included equipment fairs, health expositions, fashion and textile fairs, and pageants of cookery. It was noted that at the latter there were 7,000 people in attendance.

Recreation was stressed over the years; these community programs provided interaction that extended beyond the home and church. One of the Home

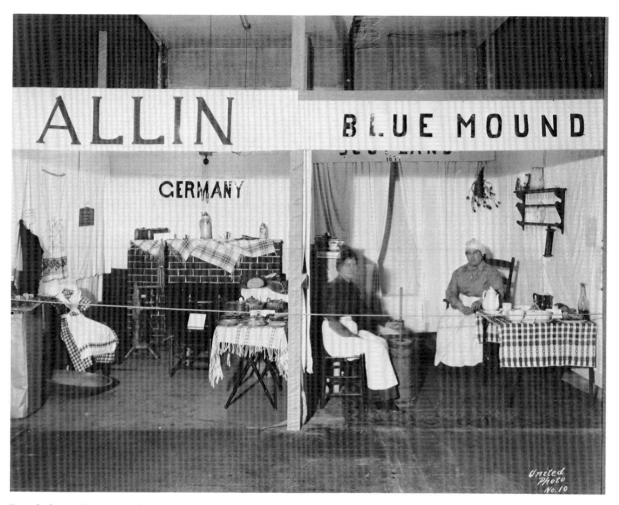

Booth from Pageant of Cookery, December, 1923

Bureau members interviewed expressed the opinion that these events broke down ethnic barriers in many areas of the county.

Remembrances of these times include the staging of plays, group singing, product exhibits, fantastic potluck meals, and much warm fellowship. More than one interviewee told of the judging that was a part of many of these events. Special mention was made by several of the soap judging which Miss Brian did. Method: place a pinch of homemade lye soap on her tongue to taste. She said that if the product was well-mixed there would be no taste of lye, and it was a very good product.

Joint Home Bureau and Farm Bureau picnics were another important event of each summer. As many as 4,000 people attended some of these gatherings.

Work with agencies continued to grow. Miss Brian designed the kitchen for the tuberculosis sanitarium, she planned menus for the Girls' Industrial Home, and helped in time and motion management with the YWCA's food service. Literally, she was an adviser to all the people of the county.

Miss Clara Brian and the McLean County Home Bureau were a well-matched team.

Home Bureau Picnic, Money Creek township, c.1920

Involving the Youth

The earliest extension work done with youth was with summer programs. This involved hiring a person to work with the young people.

Mrs. Lucille Hartzold of Danvers remembered being part of a good-nutrition pageant that was taken to the state fair. Each of the girls was dressed as a vegetable, and they participated in a large parade while there.

Miss Brian noted in her personal diary: "I find I organized the first 4-H girls' club at Towanda on July 8, 1918 and on July 11 organized a girls' club at Downs with fourteen members."

In the first year 17 clubs for girls were organized, with sewing, canning and bread-making the areas of study. Some of these club members went to the state fair and earned blue ribbons, and Dorothy Basting won a trip to the national stock show at Chicago.

With these accomplishments as a beginning, the youth program grew steadily and expanded phenomenally. By 1922, the girls' 4-H Club work was well underway.

Some time after her retirement, Miss Brian wrote:

"If I were to analyze the value of extension work the first place perhaps would be given to 4-H Club work. However, without the broadening knowledge which extension work has given to adults, there would not be the sympathetic understanding between parents and youth for their work. 'The youth of today is the nation tomorrow.' "

The first 4-H Club fair was held for a few hours the afternoon of September 19, 1919, in connection with the McLean County Breeders' Association. There were 22 exhibits.

The 4-H Club program grew and the fair grew over the years. This was, and still is, the only fair held in McLean County. The spotlight is on youth and their accomplishments.

Conclusion

In reviewing her achievements during the 25 years she worked in McLean County, Clara Brian must have had deep feelings of accomplishment. Sometimes she spoke of these in her reports, but she always acknowledged that she also had disappointments and she felt shortcomings in reaching goals and satisfying needs.

At the end of her second year of work she told of long hours, hard trips, and over-fatigue. She acknowledged that she felt discouragement and a sense of having done three women's work while giving unsparingly of herself.

When she retired in 1945, she looked forward to joining the Home Bureau and to have some time for things she was not able to do during her working years.

A more poetic view of her life as home adviser was written after her retirement:

> "Home Economics Extension work is difficult physically and mentally, but it is not monotonous. There are at least two ways by which you can enter a town. There are many beautiful trees along the way—stately and defiant in the winter time, lovely and beckoning in the summer time. There are many beautiful birds and in parts of the county bright colored pheasants are a common sight, while the finest of livestock dot the landscape in every direction. Also, so many thank you's and well wishes that one forgets one is weary."

Perhaps her most eloquent words about her 25 years of dedicated and untiring service to the people of McLean County are from her annual narrative report for 1925.

"Seven and one-half years continuous extension work in one county and I am asked to put on paper the results. Looking back on that period of time, I must ask myself has it paid? Are the results worth the hardships endured, the cold drives, the undesirable roads? The social isolation? The material sacrifices (for I have refused three offers where salary would have been better) and what is to show for those 7½ years' work?

I. A countywide group of women who have a larger circle of friends and acquaintances.

II. Better understanding of the homemaker's responsibility to her family, regarding foods.

III. Much more fruit, vegetables and milk used in the daily menu and a safer use of meat.

IV. Much more thought given to the feeding and care of the infant and run-about child.

V. Hot lunches in school, a better health condition in rural schools and less malnutrition among grade pupils.

VI. A broader knowledge of health conditions and more respect for individual health.

VII. Better equipped kitchens and more labor saving devices in the home.

VIII. More time given by individuals to community activities, such as programs, plays, recreation, etc., that are enjoyed by all the members of the family.

IX. Better color combinations in personal adornment as well as interior furnishings.

X. A group of mothers willing to spend one day each month on child study in order to know more about the physical, mental and spiritual development of their children.

XI. A safer and saner knowledge of Life Problems, and how to impart the information to younger members of the family.

XII. A larger number of women who chum with the children, who take time to look up at the stars, to laugh, to pray and to be happy."

What more revealing words can be offered? It seems appropriate that her images which depict the work and people about whom she wrote are presented here to take you a step beyond her vision of success, for her qualities of greatness shine through in the universal interests and concerns she expressed on film.

Canned foods

Photography

Capturing images on film was an early interest of Clara Brian's. At home in San Jose, photography was a hobby which became a lifelong passion. Her nephew Fred remembers looking through thousands of photos, many of them of outstanding quality, when the family closed her home in 1970.

Apparently, however, photography ranked behind her primary goal of attending Illinois Wesleyan University, for it is thought she sold her photographic equipment to pay for her first semester's tuition.

When she acquired new photo equipment is not known, but in one of her reports she commented that she never went any place in the county without the camera. Her first annual report to the University of Illinois Extension Service was liberally illustrated with photographs and captions.

The following year she began to gather photos to use in a lesson on household equipment. Illustrations of both good and bad home and farm situations were organized into an 80-count slide presentation.

When interviewing county residents about Clara's photography, the usual response was something like, "Oh yes, she was always taking pictures." Likewise, when asked why they thought there were so few pictures of Miss Brian, their comment was that she was most often behind the camera.

Photography was integrated with her professional career, and still it remained a hobby. She was an active member of the Kodaroamers of Bloomington-Normal for many years.

Among the Home Bureau files is an interesting committee report. It would appear to be a copy of findings of a committee which was presented to a professional organization. It is without a date or organizational identity, but it is well worth presenting here.

Report of Committee on Camera
Resolved—That the camera is a help to the adviser:
1st.—In getting her people interested in Home Bureau work.

2nd.—As a means of visualizing important phases of the work.

3rd.—By making comparisons of good and bad features in equipment, arrangement, yards, gardens etc.

4th.—As a means of keeping a permanent record of interesting events, places etc. and using them in future work.

5th.—Slides made from local subjects give variety and is a good way to illustrate a talk on important topics.

Clara R. Brian
McLean County
Mary Hooper
Williamson County

This report was either prophetic, or it was a summary of the ways she used her camera.

This presentation of a select few of the images recorded during the productive years of her career is a means of visualizing important phases of her work.

References

Brian, Clara R., *Biographical Sketch*, unpublished, 1957.

Brian, Clara R., *McLean County Home Bureau*, unpublished.

Kaiser, Gertrude E., *A History of the Illinois Home Economics Program of the Cooperative Extension Services*: Dissertation, University of Chicago, Chicago, IL, June 1969.

McLean County Home Bureau, *Twentieth Anniversary Cook Book, 1918-1938*.

McLean County Home Bureau Collection, 1917-1945, McLean County Historical Society, Archives.

Rasmussen, Wayne D., *Taking the University to the People*: Iowa State University Press, Ames, Iowa, 1989.

Thompson, Dave O., Sr., editor, *Five Golden Decades, 1914-1964*, McLean County Farm Bureau, 1964.

Wheeler, Adade Mitchell with Wortman, Marlene Stein, *The Roads They Made, Women in Illinois History*; Charles H. Kerr Publishing Company, Chicago, Illinois, 1977.

Interviews with the following conducted by Margaret Esposito, Summer-Fall 1989

Mr. Fred Brian
Clara Dodson—Money Creek
Marie Forrest—Bellflower
Gertrude Grimes—Blue Mound
Ruth Hamm—Hudson
Ruth C. Harrold
Lucile Hartzold—Dry Grove
Violet Hefner—Lexington
Agnes Huth
Francis Johnson—Normal
Marie Killian—Money Creek
Erlma Kraft—Normal
Alice Mohr—Normal and Money Creek
Mable Munster—Randolph
Anna Percy—Old Town and Eastsiders
Gladys Rhoades—Hudson
Mabel Ropp—Dry Grove
Minnie Weidner—Blue Mound
Doris M. Wissmiller—Blue Mound

The Photography of Clara R. Brian

Edited by Tona Schenck

"Man's method."
Horse-powered corn elevator, Lexington township, 1919

"Water is heavier than corn."
Lexington township, 1919

37

Milk, c.1920

Farm girl, c.1920-25

A boy and his pigs, c.1920-25

Farm children and pony cart, c.1920-25

"Pets." Mrs. Wakefield, Randolph township, 1919

Old woman, c.1925

Family and their lambs, c.1920

Farm children and their pets, c.1920-25

Old woman, c.1930

Children at chicken nests, 1920

Shed-style poultry house, 1920

Chicken yard and tile poultry house, 1920

Movable hog-house
(McLean County Swine Sanitation System),
c.1920-30

Sow and piglets, c.1920-30

Watering stock, c.1935

Farmer and sheep, c.1925

Unit meeting on chickens, c.1918

Unit meeting and out-door cooking, c.1920

Outdoor canning, c.1920

Woman displaying her canning, c.1930

Canning equipment, c.1920-30

Well-box for cooling food, 1920

Well-box for cooling food, 1920

Kitchen with "dumb waiter" basement cooling box, c.1920

Built-in ice box, c.1920

Kitchen shelves, c.1920

Efficient kitchen, c.1920-25

"Hot Blast" stove and "Quick Meal" stove, 1919

Efficient kitchen, c.1925

Kitchen layout, c.1920-25

The Chambers gas stove, c.1920-25

Kitchen cabinet, metal "Hoosier" type, c.1925

"Quick-Meal" stove and pressure cooker, c.1920

"Kitchen sink too low," c.1920

"Sink in center of kitchen." Home of Mrs. Lantz,
White Oak township, 1919

Kitchen with stool and carpet for stress reduction,
c.1920

New kitchen cabinets, 1919

111

Kitchen of Mrs. Carl Freitag,
Allin township, c.1935

Room arrangement, c.1920-25

Hot water for bath, c.1920

Urban poverty in Bloomington, c.1935-40
("Sanitation pictures")

Back-house and catalogue, c.1920-30

Out-buildings, c.1920

Recess at Benjamin F. Funk School,
Funks Grove township, 1919

Brush College and storm cellar,
Arrowsmith township, c.1930

Cold lunch, c.1920

Barnes School, Towanda township, c.1920

Rural school class, c.1930

Benjamin F. Funk School and grounds,
Funks Grove township, 1919

Farm children in school, c.1920

Rural school

"Duck duck, goose goose" c.1920

Rockford School, Anchor township,
with hot lunch equipment in background, 1919

School with indoor privy addition, c.1930

Lunch time, c.1920

Kitchen converted from cloak-room
for hot lunch program, c.1925

"Hot lunch equipment furnished by Community Club."
Pickett School, Normal township, 1919

Lunches served, c.1920

Twins in summer dress, c.1925-30

"These are why all the things that we do
are worthwhile," c.1920

"Homemade 'Kiddie Coop,' Mrs. Jones,
Randolph township." 1919

School children, c.1930

Playing "catch" in the farm-yard, c.1920

Rural children, c.1920

At a picnic, c.1920

Home Bureau picnic, Money Creek township,
c.1920

Kick-ball, c.1920

Unit meeting at West Twin Grove Church, 1920

"Elm tree on West Market Street Road—Summer,"
c.1920-25

View from Stewart farm, Randolph township, c.1925

"Elm on West Market Street Road—Winter,"
c.1920-25

Storm damage at Conley's, c.1934

"Serving lunch after storm at Conley's," c.1934

Burning a house, c.1935

Urban poverty in Bloomington, c.1935-40
("Sanitation pictures")

Urban poverty in Bloomington, c.1935-40
("Sanitation pictures")

Urban poverty in Bloomington, c.1935-40
("Sanitation pictures")

Safe water inspection by representative
of Illinois Department of Public Health, c.1925

"Thor Electric," c.1922

"She sits and sews while the washer goes"
(Household equipment exhibit, c.1922)

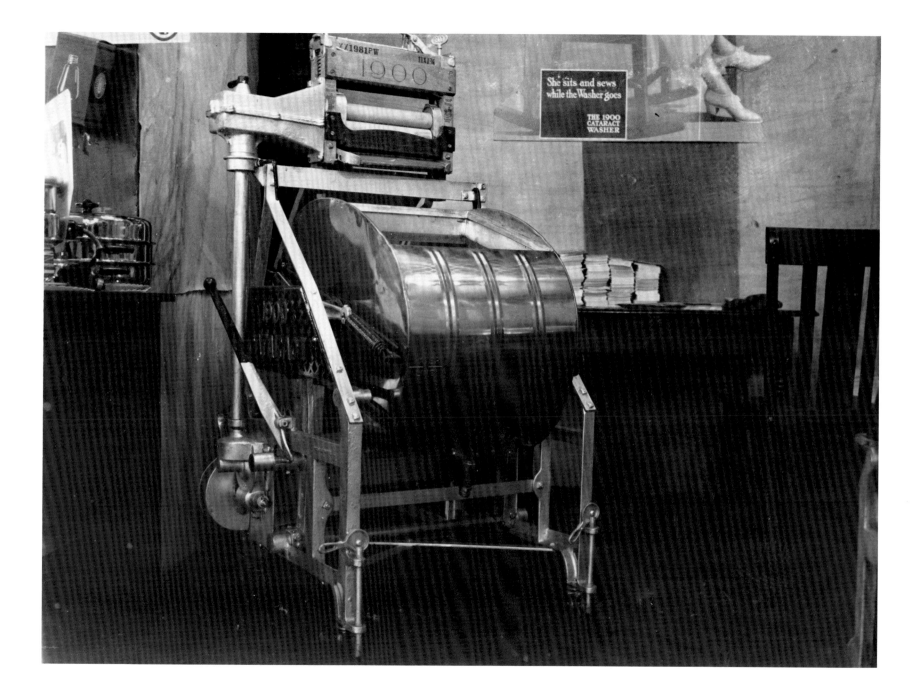

Sewing machine clinic, c.1935

Club girls and their work, 1922

4-H girls and their projects, c.1936

"Packing lunch for 4-H Achievement Day,"
c.1935-40

"Wheel tray. Mrs. Burtis, Gridley township." 1919

Table setting, c.1920

Table setting, dining room of Mrs. Thayer,
Chenoa township, 1919

Old woman, c.1930-35

Home entertainment, c.1920-25

Unified interior, c.1925

217

Farm house study, showing location of kitchen, dining room, and parlor, c.1920

"Home of Mrs. Whitesell, Empire township." 1919

Modern farm house study, c.1920

Modern farm house study, c.1920

Modern farm house study, c.1920

Mr. & Mrs. Spencer Ewing's prairie-style house,
Bloomington, c.1920
(John S. Van Bergen, architect, & Jens Jensen,
landscape architect)

229

Mr. & Mrs. Spencer Ewing's prairie pool,
Bloomington, c.1920
(John S. Van Bergen, architect, & Jens Jensen,
landscape architect)

Home Bureau leaders, c.1935
(Seated in center: Mrs. Spencer Ewing, left,
and Clara Brian, right)

Gazeball in yard of Mrs. Frank Palmer,
McLean, c.1925

Buying farm-account book from Miss Bird, c.1940

Reading *Heidi Grows Up*, c.1930

Farm woman, 1940

Home Bureau camp, c.1925

Mrs. E. D. Lawrence doing farm accounts,
Dry Grove township, c.1935

Three generations, c.1920

"Fire place of Mrs. Ambrose, Hudson township."
1919